Copyright© 2016 Spiritscribe Publishing

No part of this publication may be reproduced, stored in a retrieval system, or transmitted in any form or by any means, electronic, mechanical, photocopying, recording, scanning or otherwise, except as permitted under Section 107 or 108 of the 1976 United States Copyright Act, without either the prior written permission of the Publisher, or authorization through payment of the appropriate per-copy fee to the Copyright Clearance Center, Inc., 222 Rosewood Drive, Danvers, MA 01923 978-750-8400, fax 978-750-4470,or on the Web at www.copyright.com. **Send requests to the publisher for permission.**

The Released: A Collection of Poetic Experiences
Shiarnice T. Taylor a.k.a. Lyric the Poet

In loving memory of

Joseph Michael Barriere, Sr.   We miss you. We love you, and when we get to Heaven, we will be searching for you.

Sunrise October 26th 1926- Sunset August 31, 2013 at 11:05pm

Credits

Illustrated by: Jasmin Richard

Photograph by: RJay Jones

Facebook: Lyric Shiarnice Taylor

Instagram: lyric_the_poet

Foreword by Nikki Taplin

YouTube Channel: Lyric the Poet Shiarnice Taylor

https://www.youtube.com/channel/UCTHt1p5byje56cXykFl7dPg

Acknowledgments

There are so many people in my life that God has purposely placed in my life to speak to me, directly or indirectly. They are my angels, my family, my friends, my spiritual village, my life experiences, my moments of being hard-headed, my rebellion against God, and my poetic mentors. I thank you first and foremost, God. Without you, I am nothing. I thank you, my Mother, my Grandmother, my Aunt, my Brother, and my Stepfather. There has never been anything I was afraid to tell you all in fear that you would leave me, and you have not left my side yet. I thank you, my Great Grandmothers who, by the Grace of God, are still alive and well, lighting the ancestral path when I am in darkness. I thank you to all my family from Louisiana and for my Cajun roots: I'll never forget where I came from. I thank you to my spiritual sister, Queen Nikki aka Fertile Spirit who always has a way of explaining things to make sense, for helping to guide me, and direct me when I want to go left you steer me right. I thank my A-1 since day one Dallas Williams: even when we are distant, we are still so close; our souls are connected and I thank you for supporting me since we became friends back in fifth grade. I love you, girl! I thank you, my rock, my only tall friend, and best friend Mari Petteway. You have always been my backbone even when you may have felt I did not see you. I always saw you. I looked up to you in ways you cannot even imagine. I thank you my spiritual village Fallbrook Young Adult Ministry for giving me my spiritual wings of maturity and for helping me grow in God's word, every day. I thank you for my continued growth and showing me an example of true submission to God. I thank you my poetic mentors Nikki aka Fertile Spirit, Baritone, Rain the Poet, Savannah Blue, Khalid the Future and Poetry or Die, Jem, Brandon Jackson, God's Gift aka TJ, Brother Ced, G.O.D. (Gifts of Direction) Choice and Royal Acid love you guys. I have a special thank you to my cousin Jasmin Richard for creating an amazing cover for the book. I thank you my therapist for helping me see that my anxiety is fear that can only be overcome by staying in uncomfortable situations to help make us better people. I address all of the readers who maybe struggling with a stronghold you think you cannot overcome. You can, you will, accept who you are, love who God created you to be and submit to life to Christ and Release!!!!

To anyone who has ever struggled with anxiety, depression, or mental illness, I see you.

I hear you. I am you. Know there is freedom from your mind in Christ Jesus, and that he has sent angels to help you make it through.

You can let go, let God, and Release!!!

Foreword

There will be no dark corners of your being left when you finish reading *The Released* by Shiarnice T. Taylor aka Lyric. More than insightful and personal, Shiarnice gives you her soul in these revealing poems that exposes herself yet covers her in the Spirit and strength.

I have the privilege to know of Lyric as a young, poetic artist while sharing microphones and stages with her in Houston, Texas, but I was given the honor to really get to know her as a person and a young lady (Shiarnice) when I realized she lived in the same area as me. It all started with some ice cream at a local Dairy Queen. From there, our relationship began to grow, and I had become someone she looked up to, respected, and even sought for advice. She became like a little sister, and I knew I had a responsibility to her as a mature woman to impart tools, wisdom, and knowledge to aid in her personal growth.

Over the course of time, I could see her developing into an even better her. Shiarnice had questions I, sometimes, could not answer, but she would fearlessly embrace that approach on the matter at hand when directed to ask God or the Universe. I invite you to experience some of her experiences and even find yourself in some of these poems/stories of Shiarnice's revelations as she talks about living in the moment (Purpose), how any of us could be treated like we are "crazy" (Straitjackets), questioning our faith (Wednesday), and more. My description would only be a disservice. So, grab a cup of coffee or whatever you like to sip on while reading a good book that causes you to reflect and a quiet space because you will need. Enjoy.

Narcisse "Nikki" Taplin

Table of Contents

Part 1

Bondage

1. Straitjackets
2. Miracle
3. 22
4. Cease Fire
5. If these Walls

Part 2

Acceptance

6. Silence and Microphones
7. 4 Women
8. Anti-Stereotype
9. I am Beautiful
10. Claim it

Part 3

Submission

11. Wednesday
12. Lesson Learned
13. The Released
14. Purpose
15. Prayer Request to a Blessing
16. It's 3am
17. The Resurrection Will Not Be Televised

Straitjackets

Straitjackets are not just for the insane
but the sane. I soon realized insane
people were not the only ones trying
to harm themselves and needed restraints,
but I also, as young girl myself at the
age of fifteen, began to spiral. I thought
I knew it all and raised hell. I did not
realize my mother was trying to keep me
from going through hell and from falling
into the same concrete traps my ancestors
had walked many years back. See, I
thought I was smart. Young girls are
lusting after something to get what
their heart is missing: the whole part
of what it means to have a father, so
I hold myself tightly during this night on
unit restriction. I pray I never have to
come back to this place: Fifth Floor of
Intracare. I would remember if I ever
went crazy. No one ever called me

"crazy." I would remember if I were "crazy." The nurse even said this jacket is "too tight." "Where are my clothes? What did you do with my stuff?" I am explaining myself to a complete stranger: "I am not crazy." Nurse replies, "but you told everyone you would 'kill yourself.'" Restraints are not simply for the insane, but they suit the sane: falling head-over-hills crazy for what I think is love, wanting to die because if-I-cannot-have-him makes me crazy. At least, that is what they say as they force-fed me chicken nuggets and antipsychotics to push out verbal rejections as I lie on the cold, hard, linoleum floor. "I am not crazy!" Sometimes, you realize in desperate situations you would possibly end up on the other side of the spectrum if you did not have something holding you back like straitjackets. The probationer, and not the officer, allows anger to get the best of me, commits crimes beneath me, and uses substances as escape and addiction as an excuse. Thank God for restraints.

Adam and Eve were there from the beginning
of creation from Genesis to Revelation.
God sets limitations. We are not savages
but merely puppets of destiny. Young girls
open their legs to fill that black hole caused
by the absence of a father: the return of
never. See, he never promised you he
would love you, forever. When do we
realize the world is full of temporary
pleasures? Cutting off that hand to keep
people from stealing again will never work.
It is worthless to die before your time. So,
when I look at the nurse in this mental
hospital and tell her I am not crazy,
she replies, "But, you wanted to die." It is
a lazy excuse and an easy escape to keep
me from facing this thing we call life. Restraints
are for humanity, forcing me to love myself
because no one else could if I did not, first.
Straitjackets helped me feel my heartbeat
more than slitting my wrist and placing it
against another. I feel your pain more now
than when the blood escaped from my naked
wrist. The naked truth is that I did not

want to kill myself: it was just an excuse. Straitjackets were not only meant for the insane but also the sane as I hold my body and think of living. I began to love myself.

"Miracle"

Heartbreaks happened to her as fast as her heartbeats when she takes her first hit. It is pure in its natural form. This is the manner she was born: she was cocaine adorned, restricting the oxygen in her blood vessels. She gasped for air but none was there. She gasped for air, reached for her, but she was not there. "Clear! Clear!" We are losing your baby girl! Mother! Can't you hear her cries? She is irritable and agitated as you felt before you took that hit of white girl. "Your baby girl will not survive!" screams the doctor. "Clear! Shock! Body is going into withdrawal!" Mama! I need you to save me! Take another hit because now, without your high, I will die! Can't you see me? I know you can hear my cries soaring over your addiction like airplanes, birth pains, and poverty pains. They are aiming for your soul, to pull out guilt after

you cursed my life. Bodies are connected.
Cocaine is ingested. It is digested by our
circulatory systems. My siblings and I
share the same blood type: C positive.
How can we be positive when our bloodlines
are destined for addiction? How could
we swim in the world? Hence, you swam
to your afflictions. Listen! As my mother's
heart beats faster than mine, do not revive
something that rather fall over and die!
"Clear! Clear! I think we are losing her!"
She hears her babies crying for her while
She searches for you. The dope man is
lurking for you, waiting in the alleys. He
figures if he gets you far enough into the
darkness, you are far from reality: the reality
that your child is dying because of you, and
you are destroying lives of the other two.
How dare you eat that forsaken fruit!
She has difficulty feeding and sleeping,
and she is irritable when you stare at her
for too long. She has an enlarged head, eye,
and face (abnormalities). She cannot learn
like other children because her heart beats
faster than her brain gives her answers. She

has muscle spasms and urinary tract infections
and they are constant. The kids at school tease
her. They call her ET, but no one knows her
story. She asks her foster mother why she
was born this way, and all she can say is
"God made you this way; you are beautiful."
Although they tell her differently, she still
feels a little distant as though she does not
belong because she cannot figure out what
is wrong. Why does she not look like who
they say is her mother and father? Why does
everything she feels seem like an addiction?
Something is missing. She puts her hand over
her heart and feels it racing. Heartbreaks
happened to her as fast as her heart beats.
When her mother took her last hit in its
purest form, she tried to kill her baby that
was cocaine born. Now, she overdosed.
She cannot get a pulse. She is fading. Let
the dope man take her dreams, her life,
and her children, and oldest daughter. His
new wife's bloodlines are destined for
addiction. She swims in the world and
blames her afflictions, but she did not
know her sister survived. They thought

she died with brothers having the same blood type: C positive. They spread out but always lead back to the heart in foster homes that stretched for miles apart like veins. She wants answers, so she looks to her foster parents. They tell her she came from a lineage of cocaine pushers and poppers, and your mother tried to abort you with an overdose but failed. Therefore, we decided to adopt you because no one else wanted you: a girl with lung complications and cognitive deficiencies. You looked different from the other children. Nevertheless, we loved you all the same, so we named you Miracle because we had never seen something fight so hard against addiction. See, you overcame your affliction unlike your mother. You are a miracle: the rose that grew through the cracks of a concrete reality: an attempt at a failed abortion, AN ATTEMPT AT A FAILED ABORTION. HER NAME IS MIRACLE.

22

I close my eyes, and wish I could remember
a time when my daddy made me happy: a
time when advice was given, when a time
he hugged me so tight; I could hear when
his heart beats, not a man but a daddy
and his daughter. A father who could chase
away little knuckle head boys that grew up
just like me: empty with one man in their
hearts and memories of goings instead of
comings. Daddy, teach me to turn a blind
eye to men who prey on childhood voids,
teach me to recognize all things that seem
appealing but are meant to hurt me, teach me
the difference between love and lust, and you
must know because it is who you are, teach me
how to compare and contrast
metaphorical manipulators, how to choose life
versus what I think is love, but all you taught
me is the definition of resentment. I close my eyes,
and I can smell cologne of defeat. I close my ears
and pray I will never hear another man say
this without meaning it: "Baby, you are the only one."
I bite my bottom lip to prevent myself from

uttering "I believe you." Nothing in life hurts more at 22 than hearing moans in the distance and defeat screaming over you. He said, "baby I love you." Daddy said, "baby girl, I love you." Where were you? Victory relied on his good looks and conversation. He already had me when you left me. You never taught me how to fight against those who fill the void of a Father and crush hearts that made me crush hard for a quick second. Daddy, I thought men loved me as much as you did. Men who crawled up inside of me and died on an unlearned heart. I was never taught this part. Nothing in life hurts more at 22 than hearing if I got it, man you can get it, too. Then, hearing you got it from him who got it from her giving it to you. Daddy, I thought you loved me. He claimed he did, too. Where were you?

Cease Fire

Taking selfies in front of a hearse
is more appealing to a group of
eighteen and nineteen-year-olds
than experiencing a Caribbean,
dance festival with their best friends.
They rather take lives than live life
 dancing, singing, and having paint
and water fights, celebrating a freedom
we often take for granted since we
were never slaves. History became
irrelevant to a generation of people
who do not even value their own lives,
 not to mention another's. Whatever
happened to having a good time and
putting on your best clothes with
your best swag instead of having
 the most powerful gat without concern
 for the rest of the generation who just
wants to have fun? We came to indulge
in a cultural experience and delight in
jerk chicken and rum punch. However,
Mr. Bombastic meets us at the door,

blaring over sound systems and gunfire echoing in the distance, instead. Fired shots resonate as everyone runs to the door to find an escape. We realize fight or flight is the only way, so I start to pray while I am crouched in a corner with my friends. I found cover, as a stray bullet could have left me shot in the head and laying dead in a bull pit dead. Somebody lost a son, a brother, a nephew, a cousin, and a friend, and these fools are taking selfies in front of an ambulance. The shooter might as well have handed them the gun, and they pulled the trigger with every flash and flicker of a picture. Do you see we are killing each other with selfies? We are taking our own lives as the brother who struggled to stay alive, and those medics fought to save his life. We took selfies with blatant disrespect for someone else's son. Joseph Kony is hiding, and they still have not been able to find him. Now, children are raiding, raping, and pillaging through villages in Uganda and Sudan as Kony sips tea through umbrella straws like Kermit the frog saying, "That ain't none of my business." People in America are folding their arms and shaking their head like "yea that's sad." Child soldiers start mass genocides, but "that ain't none of our business." Europeans are too busy bantering about the Duchess of Cambridge: "what she is wearing?" and "Is she having a new baby?" Have you seen the news, lately? Rebels are assassinating villages and taking our black queens in Nigeria. Kony is starting wars against his own people, and he is not even here to see them fight. Talk about a coward creating child soldiers, brain washing the whole generation of African men, but where are our leaders? We are our leaders. Yet, we approve killing our own people because we are not worried about the African, only the African American where our children only worry about going to school, not having to fight. We are supposed to be living better: "America, the land of the free, home of the brave," and we cannot even do that right. It is a sad day in Uganda as people collect the remains of their family and friends, but it is a happy day in America when Kim Kardashian starts a new fashion trend! We are in trouble! Our black children are no longer growing up wanting to be doctors, lawyers, writers, business owners, but instead they just want to be alive. "We just want our babies to live past twenty-five." Now, society considers our communities black-combat war zones where white, racist police officers play target practice in front of our homes. Someone kills another black boy, and I cannot say I am surprised. They were born into a world learning how to survive from birth. If I had a son, my message would simply be to stay out of a police officer's way. I would tell him this, everyday, but this is still not good enough because some of us live next door to police officers. Some of our children walk to school where they patrol, and the only way to stay out of their way is to be inexistent, but as a black race, we refuse to stay out of your way. We will procreate, and I encourage our black boys and girls to get in your way, educate themselves, and take your job away because obviously when you heard the words "protect and serve," you thought that referred to you. Well, I hate to inform you, but that slogan refers to us, NOW. Protect and Serve us. Cease Fire. Our hands are up, surrendering. DON'T SHOOT!

If These Walls

If these walls could move, they would crumble, hoping someone would walk around them like the walls of Jericho. Then, they will fall. If these walls could destroy, they would destroy you. If these walls could seclude, they would seclude you by yourself, closing you inside of the cage that you created for us. If these walls had emotions, they would scream and cry for hope frantically because none exist within them. If these walls could flee, they would run for their lives, getting far away from you as they possibly could. If these walls could see, they would see a dysfunctional establishment, which is meant to be a family. They would see the laughter fading away and see a mother on her knees, begging forgiveness for sins her husband committed. They would see a baby and a girl. The baby is crying for anything that will alleviate the screaming heard from two, arguing parents. The girl locked in her room writes suicide notes of poetry. A man has esteem so low; it could cut through the breaking point of a woman, so strong but obviously now is so weak. A mother cannot bear to fight anymore because anemia, anxiety, and beatings have overtaken her. These walls feel these beatings, and they are weeping for a family entrapped in an abusive fire. Because these walls cannot move, cannot destroy, cannot seclude, talk, hear, see, nor flee. All they can do is stand while a mother gets slapped against them as a child lies within wailing. A young girl writes her last diary entry of suicidal poetry, and she slits her throat, spilling blood on these walls that can only stand as the mother wipes her face, ices her eye, and gets ready for work. She leaves these walls that can only stand because she never speaks. These walls surrounding her pray for his family that

can only live and only leave for daily,
domestic affairs while he has affairs in
a bed of a promise to love, protect,
honor, and be loyal to a wife whom
he beats, now. If these walls could
destroy, they would destroy his power
and cripple him as he has crippled his
family, leaving them longing for money
he now provides. If these walls could
speak, they would say help these people
who have loved and honored this family
since day one. If only she had not spoken
back to him at the laundry mat that day
and listened to unfulfilled nothings he
whispered to her. These walls would
not exist, and there would be no need
for this poem. There would be no baby...
no mother who has pushed passed the
walls and escaped the harsh realities
that a family can exist, and a girl who
did not commit suicide, but now exists
and tells this story that these walls
could not witness to, for I am the wall
and this is my story!!!

Silence and Microphones

Microphones were not loud enough
to carry the burdens of a soul so big
and yet so quiet; it disappears in the
middle of crowds. I search to find my
voice, but people will never hear it.
I fear it will be a whole eternity before
anyone ever notices me, silenced by
sirens of political poetry. The love of
poetry interrupted by any chance to
make a dollar. Lord, do not let me die
a martyr to a world that never understood
lessons learned. I want to die as a
lyrical assassin, gripping microphones
that drip with pain, that drip with love,
that drip with tears soaked in experience
and silenced by audiences that only anticipate
the next words. Silence me with applause
and sobs of an audience with true
understanding of what it means to be
a poet!!! Microphones were never
loud enough for Real Poets!

4 Women
Inspired by Nina Simone

"My skin is black."

"My arms are long."

"My hair is woolly."

"My back is strong."

"Strong enough to take the pain."

"inflicted again and again."

"What do they call me?"

"My name is AUNT SARAH."

"My name is Aunt Sarah."

"My skin is Yellow."

"My hair is long."

"Between two worlds I belong."

My father was rich and white."

"He forced my mother, late one night."

"What do they call me?"

"My name is Siffronia."

"My name is Siffronia."

Should I accept black or fight for white

because back in the 70's it would have

been hard enough for blacks to believe

I am black being this light.

Should I respect my heritage or submit
to the world? Here is where the confusion
lies, now. Among our black young girls, it
is hard enough fighting against the outside
world. Now, we are fighting each other over
what is all texture perspectives neglected
by accusations that your hair is too nappy.
It needs that creamy relaxant to be
beautiful these days. It is all about
them milky waves. Long weaves down
to my behind, staring at my behind, my
hips, my lips back to my behind. Black
women better get in line and stop allowing
other people to define our black. I do not
know about you, but my black has always
been enough, even back then when things
were rough. We were naturally beautiful,
rocking corn rows and afros like Nina Simone,
Angela Davis, Elaine Brown, and Assatta Shakur.
Surely, these 4 women can teach us to accept
ourselves, our black, and our hair.

Anti Stereotype

I am not a typical woman for what makes
me prized. I am a black woman I am not your
typical type of black woman, for what
brings me value I am a black woman with
class, style, and poise and I delight in
the fact that I am the anti stereotype.
See, I rely on my education instead of
my looks and choose to keep my
head in books to earn my keep. I
understand if a woman does not work,
she does not eat. Maybe, this explains
why some of these video vixens are so
skinny, relying on only beauty, not brains
gives some men the indication we as
black women are gold diggers;
moreover, since I am the anti stereotype,
I understand being a stereotype is not
about to earn me six figures. Because I
am a woman for what makes me prized
is that I am a black woman dealt the same
hand of cards as some of these other women
only difference is I reside with Kings and

Queens while you are playing with hearts, wanting diamonds, hope you get lucky off of 4 leaf clovers taking another woman's left overs while I am over here playing spades you playing pity pat I ain't got time for you Jokers. Let me show you the math of an anti-stereotypical woman like me. Grew up with one parent, which was my mother, absent father, have two degrees: one in Criminal Justice and the other in Psychology. Got 3 names I call on when I am in distress: the Father, The Son, and the Holy Ghost. Plus, I have 4 things to be thankful for: My Lord and Savior, my family, my career, and my atypical status of being a black woman who is the anti stereotype. I am everything that God created me to be. Are you?

I Am Beautiful

Despite what others believe,
I am the contrary; the epitome of
Beauty, and if looks could kill by
looking at me, you would drop dead
because I am drop-dead gorgeous
with no make-up and all because I
believe that natural is beautiful and
I wear it well. I do not need a man
to tell me what God tells me when
he looks at me. I never needed a
man to validate my beauty. The
sweet nothings he tells me are
only minor spices added to a
gumbo of ego that you do not
want to stir. I am beautiful.
I do not have to wear short shorts
or push-up bras to feel beautiful
Because my intellect enhances
my natural beauty, and if he
is a good man, ladies, he is
trying to open your mind and
not your legs because you are

beautiful. Every aspect of who you are from your kinky hair down to your feet, so walk in your beauty and never settle for less because compromise leads to corruption and if you compromise too much of yourself, you will lose your identity. Do not struggle with thinking you are beautiful: know it and show it. Flaunt it and walk in God's favor knowing that because you are beautiful despite society's standard. Raise the bar and show people how to treat you, and walk in your beauty….

Claim It

My father never claimed me. Later, he named me mistake, but seeing that God created me, I know I came from somewhere. To say without proof or evidence that something is true, he claimed, I looked nothing like him. So, my name must be Change because that's what he was afraid of. He never showed me he loved me through a kiss or a hug. Through the scope of violence, disease, and dope, we strive to birth healings. Healing from the acute pain of migration from Fifth Ward to Acres Home: two hoods that did not mix like oil and water. Mama cried more than she ate. She had no choice but to lose weight. "Sell outs" they called us, but we maintained, and out of the drought we came and declared to make it rain, and we had fun while it lasted thinking we would not have to face the music.

Happiness came and the devil claimed
temptations. Temptations ordained me
and declared my past was history,
laying the foundation for legions and
Lucifers within my skin setting a new
trend of depression. I attempted
suicide, claimed I had nothing to live
for saw cutting as a way to give more.
Because, like my father, I blamed myself.
Inwood North Insane Asylum claimed me
and rename me Unit Restriction. Crying
out to God to rescue me he showed what
a blessing I was by vicariously speaking to
me. The devil told God he had not patent on me,
so he disdained me, renaming my destiny
calling me a H-O-E (Spelled out) that could
have had H-I-V (Spelled out) potentially my
reputation displayed me as less than a young
lady. I sinned because the devil claimed
power over me but God saved me and
declared my name was victory!!!

                        You gotta claim it!!!
                        You gotta claim it!!!

Lesson Learned

My life is uncertain of what

is and what could be when

we made love on satin sheets.

Now, my heart beats like

a woodpecker's beak. My life

is now in jeopardy as this

chemistry grows more and more,

and I keep trying to ignore the

signs of why God is telling

me to leave you alone, to leave

these types of situations alone,

but I keep thinking I am grown.

I should have listened. Now, I am

on my own.

WEDNESDAY

I used to hate Sundays. I could never figure out why my worship was never worth it by Wednesday. I could never quite understand why I would go to church and leave out the same way that I came until Wednesday. I had no choice but to feel different, stop living in ignorance, and understand what I was doing from Friday to sometimes Sunday was always my weakness.
It was Halloween, and I met you at a spot never too familiar to my memory. I am not the kind of girl who would take sin off the dance floor and into sheets, but you seemed to sweep me off my feet. You were tall, bald, and muscular. I was timid yet bold with my body and vulnerable in my spirit, not listening with no intentions of what could happen next. It was Saturday, and I was courageous with curiosity of what it would feel to have my emotions rest on your chest, just to feel wanted only to be

haunted by a phone call from you on Monday. You treaded perturbed in your words. Something was wrong. You explained your private area pained you as though being stabbed in your private for 24 hours. This could not have been within a span of twenty-four hours. Urinating blood is not a symptom of amazing sex: it is the after effect of unprotected sex with the infected you neglected to tell me something was wrong. It is Wednesday and what happened Saturday is not over. Memories haunt the hallways of my body, and I'm just getting the note left on the refrigerator. Apparently, I have Chlamydia. It takes two pills to heal from lies but 4 years to heal your spirit. I still hate Sundays because everybody dresses up for church to cover up sinful Saturdays. I could never quite understand why I would go to church every Sunday and leave out the same way: empty. It is Monday again and loneliness does not sleep. I missed him. Who could have known that POF could lead to such dialects exchanged between bodies? However, this has to be real and he is surreal, so ideal; we dwell for hours inside of hell. We are addicted to heat, and I am enamored in our could be's, thinking he loves me. However, love does not live in addiction. He is infectious, literally, so we connected. Who knew POF's could lead to sudden deaths?

It is Wednesday, and my arms miss his embrace. My eyes crave the gaze of a lion drinking water and following an antelope. I took off from work just to feel sane, again. I am crazy for him, and he runs from commitment. Nevertheless, voicemails from doctors haunt the corners of his memory. He calls to tell me he has herpes. It is Wednesday at 9pm, and there are no CVS's or Walgreens carrying STD tests. My doctor's office is closed. I am pained with regret, guilt, shame, and sin of all the things I did back then. Sundays were never good enough for worship. Salvation is something I never deserved. No words can wash away the cancerous stains left on my spirit, but nothing replaces the feeling of redemption after finding out my body is disease free, knowing His blood can wash away every sin committed on a Saturday. Wednesday humps can never be climbed over until Saturdays suns/sins are forgiven. Jesus, can you ever forgive me for never listening to you? Sunday through Sunday to make it to Wednesday where I never have to hear from haunted halls reminding me of haunted falls I want to get up walk into Sunday proudly facing grace and mercy salvation is only 4 days away, and I am two steps from eternity. Wednesday is now just another day, and I am no longer, watching Sunday's sins rise over shameful skies. I cannot wait until Sunday.

The Released

Imagine there is a fire in a building filled with people. There are no stairs, no ladders, no elevators, and no fire escapes, just locked doors and one window. However, you are on the nineteenth floor of this building. As the smoke begins to fill the room, you begin coughing to the point of suffocation. The flames begin to rise and dance like crashing waves onto wooden, floorboards. Regardless of where you step, jump, or run, they are there, following you, and you will surely be burned. What would you do with just you? No smoke alarms or detectors exist to warn anyone of your pain. From a stranger's view, you are a walking building in flames. Smoke billowing inside of you. Your mouth is acting as a chimney where smoke and steam can partially escape the gaping hole in your heart, and you are

trapped inside of yourself without an
exit. How do you release? How would
anyone know or understand volcanic
eruptions inside of your heart to bring
you out of the ashes of agony? How
could anyone ever know how it hurts
so good to have your flesh burning
on the inside and your outsides glowing
like a jack o' lantern that has been
cut, carved, hollowed out, and penetrated
without your permission? Halloween
is no longer innocent when people
dress up as hope, as optimism, as
unfeasible love, liars,
hypocrites, and promises they could
not keep. How do you release? Regardless
of how many times you turn the
barrel of your .45 and you click, click,
click, you are still here, fighting in this
dying world; it makes you sick.
So, you drink, drink yourself into a
drunken stupor and get pulled over by
a state trooper, almost killing a family
of five, but God manages to keep you alive
How do you release? Do you write poems

on the walls of your heart to convince
yourself that love truly exists when, in
reality, your poems cannot fix a man
who was never ready to love you?
Nevertheless, you cannot accept reality,
so you write poems inside of your mind,
convincing yourself that you were one
of a kind when really you were one in
a million. He has hurt more people than
you. You are one of many, so you write
poems into your wrists, trying to convince
yourself that release is relief and temporary
"forevers" feel a whole lot better than
long-term "nevers." Does that really make
you whole? Have you released all the pain
out of your soul? Have you completely turned
the glass over and poured it all out until you
saw the glass half full instead of half empty?
Have you ever written poetry in your sleep,
knowing you could possibly die before you
could get out the last release? Have you
ever felt like you're moving, moving too fast,
working too much, and not praying enough,
never taking the time to put your mind at
ease? If you listen to your brain, it will remind

you to breathe, breathe. Will you make

peace with your thoughts, right your wrongs,

or accomplish the failed in heaven or hell?

Where do you choose to dwell? Will you burn

up inside or finally decide to let go and release?

Purpose

We are not savages but merely puppets of destiny.
I sat with my great grandfather at Legend of Oaks
every week on a Friday, one month ago. I brought
him a phone to place in his room as he requested.
He wanted a phone brought from his home, so I did
it because I knew how much he wanted to be home.
I tried to accommodate him with anything he requested.
We laughed about the nurses, and he complained
about going to therapy as he did on a routine
occasion. I showed him how to use the speaker
system on his phone. I called a few people he
requested to let them know he was okay: his
sister, a friend, my mother, and grandmother.
He called every number out to me as I dialed.
He knew the numbers by heart: he was still sharp
in the mind. He reminisced, as usual, about going
to VFW on Sundays in addition to how much he
missed sitting with his friends. He asked me to
bring him some coffee and an apple pie from
McDonald's, and everyone knew my grandfather
loved his coffee and his sweets. He told me I was
the joy of his day, and he never wanted me to leave

which made my day. I saw my grandfather still living
and breathing that day. His mind was more than
capable. I knew he had fulfilled his purpose in life.
He was happy, resulting in my heart leaping with joy.
Try something, one day. Try telling God your plans,
and watch him laugh because he has humor, and
a purpose for you & me. See, being alive is
being present; many people are alive, they are not
living, regretting the mistakes of tomorrow. You
cannot rewrite history; God does not give you
more time to borrow. Many people are alive, but
they are not living. They are breathing, but not
breathing life into their situations. Face it. Some
of us are like rocks with legs. We are spiritually
dead. God gives us a day and we throw it, away.
Fulfill your purpose. Remember that God's
mercies are new, everyday. Do not allow age to
make you decay. He did not age at eighty-five.
He was still driving at eighty-six. He was still
taking the bus to Coushatta every chance he
could, driving himself to Kroger (his favorite
place) and Luby's. He was still coming to see
his children on Sunday and going to church
when it was not too cold or too hot. He always
made a way. He never forgot to speak his mind,

and everyone else's, too. He would tell you like it is. If it hurt your feelings, face it. It was the truth. He taught me to live a life that is pleasing to God's sight, and remember grace and mercy will carry me a long way. We are not savages but merely puppets of destiny. So, tell me have you danced, today? Have you laughed until it hurts? Have you cried until you laughed, sung aloud as if you were in front of a crowd? Held your wife's hand like it was your last chance? Told your husband how much you love him, over and over again? Called your mother or your father? And told them how much you loved them after a big fight? As I held his hand on August 29th (two days before he passed), I whispered, "I love you" to him. "We love you," and he squeezed my hand tighter and tighter. His heart rate increased, rapidly. I know his heart beats for us...for him to show he was fighting to love, and death could not stop him. God gave him the ability to live until he was ready to make him an angel. My friends and family, learn the definition of *living*. Dance in your purpose. Do what you Love. This is not the end. This is just the beginning of our purpose.

Prayer Request to A Blessing

I dreamt about you, again: a tall,
dark, and shadowy figure. You often
appear in the hallways of my dreams
after long days of suffering. My
subconscious prays for you, the spirit,
intercedes for me even when I am asleep.
I see you in grocery stores, at gas stations,
at football games, at church, at bible study,
at poetry lounges, and even at work, sometimes.
You are so real to me although I have never
seen you. I feel as though I have always seen
you. You are something like an epiphany.
You are so real to me. You are someone I
have dreamt about and prayed to God for.
I am waiting patiently for my prayer request
to turn into my blessing. Lessons learned at
an intersection, and you stood there at the exit.
Turn right for your blessing, and I turned left
for my flesh, and I keep seeing you in my dreams.
I feel like you are praying for me as much I am for
you, and I see you standing, waiting to open the
doors of opportunity for me. Chivalry has always

been a part of you. I see you as I drive around
in other people's laughter. God always had a
sense of humor. I see us climbing stairs of faith
and watching our children play. I see us stopping
whatever we are doing just to pray that our
marriage stands the test of time. I see you
growing with me in scripture and in verse,
in rhythm and in rhyme. I see it all from
the start until death do us part.
I see myself waiting patiently, trusting God
for you. Sometimes, I do it in disbelief as
Abraham and Sarah of conceiving even in
their olden days. Our golden days spring
forth as Isaacs who grow as olive chutes.
Lord, bless me with the meekness and
unpretentious humility of Ruth. Allow me
to be ready to be the quintessential essence
of a Proverbs-30 woman for this man:
my future husband. You are so close but
so far. However, I will wait for you and
continue to pray for you, knowing that
my prayers are not in vain, because you
are the blessing to my prayer request.

It's 3am

It's 3am, and the sky is stelliferous
with God's light that shines on the
Earth. In this part of the Universe,
the sun is sleeping, waiting to be
awakened by God's command,
and you find yourself between
the sheets of an unexpected
woman or man (antipodes to this
universe). Sins are rising over
sunsets that were not rehearsed.
How common is it for you to forget
John 14:15 between *hallelujahs* and
three to four *amens*? How often do
you forget you serve a risen Savior?
If the rapture were to happen
between these hours, would he
condone your behavior? Would
you go to heaven or hell? It's 3am,
and it is crunch time in the middle of
your regrets, and you realize Heaven
has a room full of your spiritual debts.
However, Jesus nailed all your sins to

the cross, but you cannot seem to shake your inner devil off. You are holding captive every single person who ever wronged you. Your happiness cannot be released because you are a slave tomorrow. When will you realize Earth is a temporary home? You have to get it right, now. There is no more time to borrow for tomorrow. So, ask yourself is your hour worth of pleasure really making you better for an eternity in Heaven that could be forever.

The Resurrection Will Not be Televised

You will not be able to go to church.
You will not be able to proclaim the
name that is which who saved Jesus Christ.
You will not be able to stand up against
Adultery, Fornication, Lying, and Murder
because the Resurrection will not be
televised. However, Sin will become
normalized The Resurrection will not
be brought to you by CNN, MSNBC, BET
or ABC, and the FCC will no longer be
allowed to censor your favorite television
shows like *Love and Hip-Hop Atlanta,
New York, Scandal*, and *Empire*. The
Devil's too busy building armies and
empires of those who will have forgotten
about Jesus. The Resurrection will not
show you pictures of the passion of
our Savior Jesus Christ, his body beaten
wounds drawn on like a etch a sketch
blood dripping from his body every
drop shed that covers a multitude of

our sins. No, the Resurrection will not be televised. There will be no positive role models for your kids to look up to, no biblical characters to compare your life to, no miracles performed, heard, or seen. There would be no Joseph and Mary, no Jesus entering a womb of a virgin. There would be no Sarah and Abraham no Isaac, father, and mother birthing nations of Kings: No David and Goliath, no Moses and the Red Sea, no Jonah and the whale, and no Paul going to Jail. No, the Resurrection will not be televised. No images of Christ dying on the cross to save us all from going to Hell. There will be no more crosses worn around our necks as a reminder of a risen Savior. There will be no more TBN or CBN, no Tony Evans or Potters House Pod Cast played on your radio stations. No more Kernie Thomas broadcasted on BET screaming about "GODDDDD" at 3am on Sundays. No more *Dr. Bobby Jones and The Celebration of Gospel*. There will be no more mission trips to spread the gospel. Everybody will be

conforming to this world and nobody will
be transformed by the renewing of their
minds; nobody proving what is good,
acceptable, and perfect in the will of
God. Everybody will have a God, but
nobody will know Jesus!
The Resurrection will not be televised
The Resurrection will not be televised.
The Resurrection will not be televised.
There will be no reruns of the Resurrection.
The Resurrection will not be televised
until the Rapture revealed in Revelations,
and all of the blind-faith Christians will
claim to know Jesus, and he will say,
"Depart from me. I never knew you,"
and you will wish you never took a
commercial break from God.
The Resurrection will not be televised.
It will only be walked out in your life
when you understand that wearing a
cross does not necessarily mean that
you know Jesus Christ, so how can you
say you love him when you do not keep
his commandments? Turn on your television
set and tune in because this is Breaking News

that can save your life!!!!

The Resurrection has already been televised.

Author's Commentary

Straitjackets was written when I was a teenager during a time when people had a small idea of what depression and anxiety looked like but labeled everything and everybody crazy. At this time during my life, as many parents know, teenagers rebel. But I was not only rebelling against forces between my mother and the life she wanted for me, but I was also rebelling against my future. There were so many amazing things I knew people saw happening with my life; however, my vision was jaded due to wanting to be loved by someone I now understand should have been my father. At the time, he was a young man who could not give me the love I sought because it was from the wrong person. "Straitjackets" examines the need for human restraint when people still choose to obey God despite their inclination to rebel against his established, natural laws for us. This poem reminds us there are still spiritual laws and worldly laws we must follow. I rebelled against God as a child rebelling against a parent, thinking I knew it all. God gave me the option to choose life and to choose his love during moments I thought I did not want to live.

Wednesday

The most difficult poem I ever had to write was of my own testimony in the poem entitled "Wednesday." This poem takes a journey into what I call my naked truth (things that God and only I know, but I chose to bear it all). The reason the poem is entitled "Wednesday" is it seemed nothing could go right and everything that went wrong always went wrong during this portion of my life on a Wednesday. I chose to sin until I became a slave to my own sin. Sex became an addiction to me; it was a release of energy exchanged between two people who could pretend, at least for a while, we loved each other. Nevertheless, every man I had been with was truly just as broken as me. I was searching for love in places where mothers' and fathers' absences were considered normal. Everything in life has good and bad consequences. The sins I committed Monday through Friday always came back to haunt me on Wednesday, which is when I finally learned I could not keep running from God: I had truly learned my lesson from this particular sin. I still struggle with different sins, but now, I can say I am longer a slave to that particular sin anymore through Christ Jesus.

Cease Fire

A poem originally designed to be a group piece between myself and an amazing poet out of New Orleans, J Black. I decided to include this poem in my book because the topic is so prevalent in this day and time and what African American people are facing. A shooting and stabbing occurred at a well-known Caribbean Festival in Houston, Texas called Juve where two local young men were involved in an altercation with one another outside of the festival. At the door, there was no security: therefore, people were able to bring in weapons and other things that could possibly harm anyone. I watched as a young African American male stabbed and shot another young African American male. People were running and screaming "get down get down". Several people were trampled on trying to get out. Once we were able to get out I noticed something very strange about the young people around me. They seemed to be numb to their surroundings of viewing a killing that took place between two young black males; it almost seemed to be normal so much so that they were taking pictures for face book and recording what had occurred. I thought to myself why is it so easy for us to kill our own people? Yet we expect so many other races and cultures to respect us and treat us as their equals when we don't as black people see our neighbors as equals. This poem was designed to bring awareness in all aspects of people dying around the world not just for racial tension against police brutality, but also a reminder of why we have to stop killing our own people. We must understand, research, and educate ourselves to uplift one another, so that witnessing a murder of another human being is not seen as normal but as a tragic event in life.

The Released

Everybody has their something, their way of releasing pain, stress, illness, trial and tribulations through something. Whether they tell their best friend, their mother, father, sister or coworker or pray to God about it. How do we release? After experiencing so much pain in my life I turned to many things physical relief (sex/gym), emotional relief (sex/talking to friends), mental relief (therapy/counseling) but truly I had never experienced release until I submitted my life to Christ. I decided to handover all of my troubles to God, and I know it sounds cliché to pray to God about your troubles and things will go away. Technically, that is not how it works. It was only when I rebelled against God's will and bumped my head a million times until I found myself on my knees and everyone had failed me, is when I decided to look up and I prayed a prayer so long that my knees felt like wood, and I heard the voice of God say submit. So I did, and since then nothing within my scope of relief or release seemed to take the pain away like the spiritual release I had been seeking all of my life.

The Resurrection Will Not Be Televised

This poem was inspired by Gil Scot Heron's "The Revolution Will Not Be Televised." Gil Scot Heron examined the period when African Americans were experiencing great strife, racism, and biases without civil or basic rights in America. Therefore, I decided to take that concept and examine the world we are in now, and how we have taken Jesus out of this world, especially in America. This is what happens when we forget about the Resurrection of Christ. I did not entitle this poem *The Resurrection Will Not Be Televised* as a means of saying Christian people should not want to know about the greatest Sacrifice in history or to not share Christ with people who do not know him. The purpose of this poem reflects my belief of what the world's condition will become without acknowledging Christ's Crucifixion for our sins and his Resurrection, which will only become a thing we read about in history books. It will be something people will become more desensitized to than they are, presently. It is already common for rappers and media moguls to wear crosses around their necks, and people do not even truly understand the meaning of the symbol or the message it represents. What would happen if this world forgot all about Jesus? Better yet, would you want to live in a world without Jesus? What would you teach your children? What would our morals and belief system be based on without Christ and the Resurrection of Christ? When you read this poem, think about that, and if you cannot see a world without Jesus, do something about it! Change it! Start telling more people about him, and let the word of God and the Resurrection spread like wildfires.

www.ingramcontent.com/pod-product-compliance
Lightning Source LLC
Chambersburg PA
CBHW072035060426
42449CB00010BA/2273